# THE SHARK IN QUETTA
AN UNFINISHED LOVE LETTER TO A MORNING STAR

EAVAN HOWE

Copyright © 2024 EAVAN HOWE
All rights reserved.
No part of this book may be reproduced, translated, excerpted, reprinted, or adapted in any form or by any means without the written permission of the copyright owner.

Cover design: Guo Yi, Gu ZJ
Illustration: Dr. Syed Tariq Shah, Eavan Howe
Editor: David Boyle

ISBN: 978-1-957144-94-8

Library of Congress Control Number: 2024902357

Published and distributed in February 2024 in the United States

Asian Culture Press LLC
1942 Broadway St., Suite 314c,
Boulder, CO 80302,
United States

For information on reprints, adaptations, or other licensing inquiries, please contact the Author at www.eavanhowe.com

*EAVAN HOWE*
# POEMS

Dedicated to wanderers who are born in spring with an autumn soul.

The flesh, your food.

What's left, the soul

Yield to the red-painted maw

Of that voracious shark that glides

The deeps we crept from long ago.

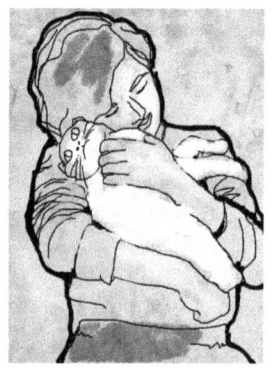

# ABOUT THE AUTHOR

Poet and novelist Eavan Howe's life story unfolds like her poetry—rich in emotion, vibrant in detail, and deeply intertwined with the beauty and pain of the world around her. Born and brought up in a quiet countryside of central China, Eavan spent her teenage years in the historic city of Xiangyang, where ancient echoes and the ever-changing dance of seasons whispered early tales into her soul.

Eavan's academic journey, encompassing undergraduate study in Jilin University and in I-Shou University, transcended a mere pursuit of knowledge; it was a voyage across varied landscapes of thought and culture. Her time in Poland, serving as a volunteer teacher of Chinese language and promoter of Chinese arts, was not just a professional endeavor but a heart-opening experience, deeply connecting her with the rhythm of distant lands.

Moving to Korea to earn her master's degree from Sungkyunkwan University, she encountered a mysterious *morning star*, a painter with rare gifts and insights. She called him "shark" "wild deer" "old neighbor". She saw his brave heart and she touched his face, she said that whoever once touched one of those orange faces, who held all the brilliant rays of sun in sky.

Besides Poland and Korea, Eavan's odyssey extended further, stretching across continents and cultures. Her life in 31 countries was not just a tally of places visited, but a kaleidoscope of roles and revelations— from the precision and creativity demanded as an automation engineer to the soul-stirring moments captured through her lens as a photographer, and the brutal business she leads as a well-rounded and cold-blooded financial expert. Also, she is a trained brewer who for three years was the owner and host of an artisan bar whose regular patrons included filmmakers, writers, musicians, artists, and poets.

Profoundly influenced by the introspective depths of *Anaïs Nin*, the poignant clarity of *Wisława Szymborska*, and the eloquent simplicity of *Elizabeth Bishop*. Eavan's writing resonates with the same complexity, depth, and emotional honesty. Her experiences—the reflective tranquillity of winter in Xiangyang, the lively bustle of Hong Kong streets, the serene contemplation in Suwon's autumn, and the spiritually rich fabric of Beirut — infuse her work with vivid imagery and evoke visceral emotions.

Eavan believes in the power of language and narrative to unveil the deepest human truths. She once remarked, *"If there were no languages, no books, then all the pasts and presents of humankind would be pallid, and so would I be to you; for the only way to be naked before you would not exist. I firmly believe so, and I write. And I believe that my whole life is but an unfinished love letter to you."*

Currently dividing her time between Hong Kong, Shenzhen, and Istanbul, Eavan Howe continues to love, extract beauty from life, and interweave the rich tapestry of her life's experiences into her writing—each word a testament to the beauty, pain, joy, and eternal longing that define the human experience.

www.eavanhowe.com

# PREFACE

*To a Shark from His Neighbor*

They asked me for drugs, I gave them letter, story, beautiful souls. And I told them about drawing, writing, mistaking and desires. I was a liar. I couldn't tell them about you, I couldn't show them your picture, your smile, the flower and the valley we saw in one secret dreamland.

For you're the rare one to me. You may say the same to me but you don't really need to, as I knew it millions of years ago, when we were stars and first met in the sky.

Writing to you, is a habit, is my life, is now. Just in the collection of poems and in your beautiful eyes, I should like to bury something precious. Then when we were old and lines on our face more marked, we could sit in a cafe somewhere together and read the poems page by page and see how a young poet once paid visit to your heart in spring.

We could come back and dig it up and remember THAT I ought to take good care of you always, as how I have been seeing to the wild orange garden of my heart.

And remember THAT it was your romantic ethos,

We celebrate, and we imagine.

Imagine how beautifully sad it is when summer meets the heart of spring, and the scorching sunshine meets rains and tears from a star I've left for long. Imagine I was there and you're here with me. Imagine that love between you and me is like a sigh, I yearn for your sighing here by my side. Sigh...

Eavan<br>
Shenzhen, 2023

# WHO SHOULD READ THIS BOOK?

This is one of the most difficult questions for any author to answer. Authors wish that every human who has ever existed should have read their book—every human that currently exists and every other that will fortunately or unfortunately make it to this world should read it. However, as an old neighbor of a poet and speaking on behalf of her, I cannot tell you who should read this book—but I am very certain about the people who should not read this book.

You should not read this book if you have not experienced a love deeper than life itself; if you have not cried in the midst of love; if you have not laughed at the craziness of love; and if you have not written a love letter.

You should not read this book if you do not long for a warm hug and a soft kiss; if you have not firmly held someone's hand in fear of separation; if you cannot read the stories that linger in someone's eyes; if you have not heard silent screams and loud whispers.

You should not read this book if you have never gone to bed hungry; if you have not stolen anything; if, besides all fears, you have not stared at life in its entirety; if you have not felt hopeless and wished for superpowers, and if you have never been on the brink of giving up, toyed with the idea of escaping life, but ultimately clung to life and fought vigorously.

This book is possibly not for you, if you are not moved by Van Gogh's Starry Night; if you have not smiled at Monet's Water Lilies; if Käthe Kollwitz's Misère didn't bring tears to your eyes. Avoid this book if you don't like to dance to music, if you don't watch movies, and if you don't read paper books.

Please, do not spend time and money on this book if you have never deeply loved; if you do not struggle to extract happiness from this fragile life; and if the intricate tapestry of your beautiful life is not woven with fear, joy, hope, tears, love, enthusiasm, ambitions, failures, and smiles – Just Don't!

An Old Neighbor<br>
Essex, 2024

# Contents

## | THE SHARK IN QUETTA |

003  In the Warmth of My Breath
004  Old Love of Mine
006  Old Poem
007  My Madwoman
008  Orange Star
011  Sapphire Blue
013  Sadness Is Also Good
014  Black Bird
016  Sleepwalker
017  My Sheltering
021  Dying, Dying, My Man Is Dying
022  Acoustic Bar (Emotion Talks)
024  The Meaning of Being Naked
026  If a Heart Could Name That Tune of Darkness
028  Give Up Feeling Heartbreak
029  Until

032  Nineteen Winters

033  Constellation

034  The Shark in Quetta

038  Birthday

039  See

040  Under Seongsu Bridge

041  Like a Certain Night

042  North Bank

## | WHITE CROW |

045  Just Before Many an Autumn

046  Recipe for Living

047  How I Do Love Thee

049  Spiral Galaxy

051  Crescent

053  A Girl

055  One Thousand Islands

057  Sugar Woman

059  To the One There

060  Green Cherries

061  Sadness

062  In My Timber's Heart
063  Orange Guitar, Green Guitar
064  How Do I Slip to This Place?
066  Love Amazes Me
067  In Her Dream
069  Sullen When a Summer
070  He Is a Boy
072  Be a Visitor
074  Name
075  Spring Fever
077  You May Just Need a Few Dollars
079  Sway
080  She Likes This Place
081  Something in
082  Su

## | MESCALERO |

085  Ice Fall
086  Prepare
090  Banana Trees
091  On the Mountain Road to the Village

092   How Are You This Night?

094   So Far, So Far

095   A Remorse

097   When It Is a Lonely Night

099   1984

100   I Want to Cry Here Every Morning

101   1982

103   As a Losing Touch

105   The Poem a City Wrote to Me

107   Beautiful, My Beautiful Woman

109   Well, Hello There

110   Elegy

112   It Was Fascination

113   It Was Fascination 2

115   With a Soul I Got Drunk

117   Cilia

119   Mescaline

120   Obsession

121   Evening

122   Marguerite

124   Autumn Equinox

125   Where Butterflies Go

*In the Warmth of My Breath*

I fold you in the warmth of my breath
In yellow bunched sunlight wrapped safe in my breast
Tucked in a long sigh.
In bittersweet dandelion wine summer-made
I hold you,
Close as a constellation.
In fragrant springs
On blind veridian forest paths
On mountains and down green glens which
We threaded long ago.
In the stills of hurrying time
In cigarette glow
With fair, clumsy words
I say you and your name trips on my parted lips.
I have you flow in crimson ink
From my blind pen
Whereafter, the false letter swept from table to floor
I dream I draw your heart to mine.

## *Old Love of Mine*

If ever you touched a lake-skin
You felt serenity, snake-smooth.
Your eyes the eyes of deer gazed at
The orange eyes of doves.
Your ears heard leopard breath, your heartbeats brave as lions'.
You swam alone into the forest deep.
Kissed the first flower of spring
Picked a dandelion gone to summer seed
Cried for an autumn leaf as it spun
Longed for the snow that started winter
Fresh on the hillside, perfect as your lover's skin.
Whenever you called me a woman of passion
You held tender and graceful this heart that still trusts.
Yet I called you only
An old love of mine.

Seagull, 2015 (Dr. Syed Tariq Shah)

*Old Poem*

Just who is this crazy guy
That I need deep breaths before seeing him tonight?
Just who is the crazy guy
That all the peace I fished will drown in big surf?
Forecast: waves, I bet they'll be blue
Singing a song, dancing along
They break.
They may break something else besides
If they don't sleeve my heart in a globe, as crazy guys do.
But just who is he?
A scar-face?
A whistler and clamberer over my groynes ?
A knower that in hot breathless summers I miss his imp's smile?
Like I miss glossy green leaves.

## My Madwoman

Goodnight, my mad woman
Take off your clothes. All
And the bonds not seen.
Drop determinations to the abyss
No longer yours. Tonight
No-one is here
No-one can hinder.
The mermaid will press them to luminous coral
Lips and keen her green sea-song
For you, my beautiful mad woman.
If they fall to the shark, why care?
Let them feed it.
Sleep now
In the garden under the Moon.
I lie at your side.

*Orange Star*

Sorry, Orange Star.
Look at me, close, hold my gaze firm.
How can I answer your questions?
I'm naïve, slow
Your scent's of cheekbone.
No. I'm scared
I'm a dove in the skylight
No intentions
Nor strength to try.
When I inhale your skin's cologne
My bird's heart chokes.
I stand still
You fragrantly kill.

Sorrow and
Regret, Orange Star.
Those burgeoning spring days
I capitulated all.

Loose your grip, I really
Couldn't say
Gift me tongues to speak
And words to spell
Wings to beat of
All my need for you.
Love me true as any can
Kiss me, blow
Your scent through my hot dreams.
Or then again
Love me hardly as you will
Know me not, know naught of me
For when I speak
You cease to glow.

South African Orange Star, 2016 (Dr. Syed Tariq Shah)

*Sapphire Blue*

How deep a sea would have to be
To bear this meek and
Quiet, morning bluntness.
How sharp a far-off sound to bear
To tear apart
This sapphire blue.

Sapphire blue
Limitless as galaxies
No scream can plumb its depths
Nor jumper's leap.
No ready compromise
But roiling destruction, recreation
Spread to me.

I see clear how shallow sick words were
How wearing
Cloying tropic rot

Still I'm breathing
Small creatures rattling
Creeping in me.

It stings.
After hers, every skin pricks.
My lips appease
Intent on thawing winter grief.
Folds of hills swell up and fall
Hiding the place to hide.

Sapphire blue.
Peering from its heart I see
Small-fish scales glinting
From a swooping seafowl's beak.
Wills tame them, never daring
To deny the night's dark lacking her
How bright my soul burns blue.

## *Sadness Is Also Good*

Sadness is also good.
The basement jazz house in that Kraków street
Where she said dying would work well there too.
Falling I'll take, through night and night
But not yet down to death.
Seeing that beauty in the drop
How could I have
My ego
And die?

*Black Bird*

A black bird stuck on rails along
The bridge I traverse every day
No black cat or black-dressed woman
It could fly, high, high away.
I saw it
And life's worries broke upon me like a wave.

I knew for sure that from then on
That all my words would grey to black
Through blue and back
And see the sea
Turn ebony.
SMH.

People rarely understand
I've walked beyond redemption's end
Slipped into the last abyss.
Books left me cold

Until she said
That I'm the book she lives to read
I should have been the first to speak
Called her *Anabasis*.


One sad song to use my opened throat
To wipe my memory clear as glass
A pebble in my shoe, I walk a few
More steps, and find and cast it
Aside, wide to the roadside
To salt deeps that my blue veins suck.
A white bird perched on dulse and rock
Scoring the waves in grey dawn light
A voiceless apparition.

*Sleepwalker*

A year's once around.
What if he sleepwalks a year, still –
He moves in dreams.
His head aches a year, still –
The ache to see again
A deer he met on fern-laced paths.
As leaves green years
Winds blow them brown.

*My Sheltering*

I'm one who cannot concentrate
My mind bewitched nine times an hour.
But paranoid for heat and scorch
Freezing ice-cold, and fantastic
Psychedelic, bitter, dark.
Monsoon rains and tropic nights
Vistas I can reach to touch.

This isn't what I thought I'd be
My heart expects to have its way
Not likely it can learn new tricks.
But there are moments when I do
Discard my jitters like a coat
And see as clear as day.

I never lack a good excuse
Answers wiggling past their questions.
Watch it, listen well, and look
With gimlet eye at what I say
No HUAC victim could touch me
For saying much and telling nil.

I know I'm feverish, crazy for
My river world, my fossil world.
I slow things down the way I like
But still, I know, I'm keen as keen
On vanities that quickly blaze.
I play, I can't see how life's grave.
Dancing women, drunken men
Colours, sleeping violet dawns
I see them all.
I'd paint but know I never will.
I hate to sleep, hate wearying

Hate summarizing summaries
Hate dreary talk of trivial things
Dull as a hair dryer's whine.
Love lovers outside
Talking of the same.

Come to me, angel.
My breeze, my fire
Come close to me.
Come to me and light the night.
Light this house, burn me bright
Burn me to the bone.
I wish, so wish that you and I
Burn to our bones together
Deaf in our carnal fire.

Monkey, 2014 (Eavan Howe)

*Dying, Dying, My Man Is Dying*

Dying
My man is dying
While I survive like a stubborn, lucky soldier
Wind-blown like low desert land.
I hold him tight
Let myself go.
Nodding flowers watched
This man's life joined with mine
And now it's done.
Him reaching still to dry my welling eyes
And touch the breast he's loved.
Flowers nod
And live and die.
Do they know who my calls will find
With him in their dark loam?

## Acoustic Bar (Emotion Talks)

Seeing that green guitar again
You say you want my heart.
You say you want to talk emotions
I say flip a coin.
If I call right
You dance with me
To that guitar's green tune.

Among the dancers
Hands clasped round
Your waist and mine
This heart of yours
So new seduced
Will beat blood in 4/4 for you
Sing springtime tunes in tune for you
Dye green as I die in green eyes.

Orange you see
Three brigands you see
Who bloom and sing no praise, you see.
Old friends of my sweet heart you see
In those emotion talks you want
Before
And now
And ever.

## The Meaning of Being Naked

If I've drunk a bucket full
If our connection's no more than
A blaze of heat at night
Would you demur?
Study my eyes.
Call me Outsider but admit
You're naked in my scorching gaze.
I'm demanding,
You're unspoiled
A tight-wound spring I'd say.
Embrace my hot delusion
I've seen you through and seen through you.
Admit I weave your heart's desire
Tempt your spirit's appetite.
You get to be what you declined
Cloves in my beer

And I bind you, soul and mind.
Get up.
Our next bottle, walk with me
Stay close, our fingers twined
I'll dream for us
Your part is just
To match your steps with mine.

## *If a Heart Could Name That Tune of Darkness*

If a heart could name that tune of darkness
What besides it couldn't see?
A heart once plunged
To the abyss
Where else it couldn't go?
A man who walked the desert place
Seeking whom he may devour
From the past and flickering now
Entered immense solitude
In faith there would be sunlight,
Food, flowers, and everything good.
There was a time that he held fast
His sense of wide ambiguous space
Now all that's gone
Leaving his heart alone in dark
But thinking still

There's will
To make a sparking fire to warm
And feed the hungry.
When he breasts the murdering Styx
My salt tears
Will teach me how
To know too well
The meaning of tomorrow.

## Give Up Feeling Heartbreak

How?
How can you give up feeling heartbreak?
This desperate will
Old world, new world.
How can you stand up
Shake off sorrow
Shrug, and walk away?
Say that spring unfolded
Beautiful and cunning
Stealing your regard.
That spring is gone
And you've not come.
Spring planted strange seeds
Deep in you
No way for you to know.
Cherish them and learn to love
The sorrows of its leaving.

*Until*

Until new notes sounded
Until footsteps slowly neared
Time deep down inside me fused and seared with yours.
Meandering river memories persisted in their flowing
And through pale pink roses
I saw you.
Lifeless long-hair woman
Sunshine, lingered nostalgia
Yawning fire-furred cat.
Seared viola prionantha
Colouring at my word.
Prosperity and satiation
Resting raindrops, green grass plots.
Flocking white doves
Caught in glass.
Breeze and shadows forest-deep

I walked in them from Fall to Yule
You said you want to walk the Year
From birth to grave with me.
Forgot, I walked alone by night
Until blown cold possessed my heart
Leaves trod in soil
Until the end at which I knew
That everything is you.

Cat, 2015 (Dr. Syed Tariq Shah)

*Nineteen Winters*

Suppose I could stay nineteen winters here
And then another nineteen springs
And you still with us living.
If one bright day sat on a bench
Among spring blooms or subway station din
I saw you pass, your face displaced
Through time and changed
How suddenly my heart would crease
And how soon it would smooth.

*Constellation*

The Greeks joined up the starry dots
To make the Big and Little Bears
And Zodiacs at their stations
They did a bang-up job of it.
Not one dark spot, no vacant lot
For one more constellation.

If even one Hellene had had
A cataract or lazy eye
Or couldn't stand to look quite through
A busty nymph on fluted plinth
There'd be a scrap of empty sky
For Constellation You.

I'd stake our claim where he stopped short
And thread the unclaimed stars to set
Your essence high above
Crossing meridians with the Moon
Until the hurtling Earth and Sun
Are far from what we love.

*The Shark in Quetta*

In sixty-seven's waning spring
White jasmine, lilac, early blooms,
My narcoleptic botanist
Slept through Hyacinth's soft kiss.

The guitar player broke his arm
The drunken poet cracked his head,
Ah, no —— the temple of his art ——
And every novelist healed up.

We swallowed too much aitch too oh
And beached ourselves on stove-hot sand
Our plan, to soon evaporate
The brine we'd shared with littorals.

Seven hundred clicks' hot land
Between us and the nearest sea
She said, it sounds so far away
But have you ever stopped to think ——

The soul inside that lights your eyes
Can loop our Earth full ten times round
Before the clock ticks one, two, three.
Such freedom. Where's there left to go?

We saw then with our land-locked eyes
What happened twenty years ago
Was yesterday, the plots contrived
By novelists, countless tides before ——

Chan' Pozzo's congas thrummed and shook
For Dizzy's high, brass-wailing horn.
Four Bretons and their honking geese
Danced welcome for a poet strange.

As clouds drooped down to join the sea
Stretched on a tide-ribbed beach we felt
Pressed to the ocean's soundless floor.
She said, life surges turbulent here ——

Churning, looming like rogue waves.
If down below, we meet again
By treasure-chests and octopi
Be shark-swift, please, don't hesitate.

Twist like mako, tiger-fierce
Bluefin-savage, thresher-cruel
Turn your doll's eyes into mine, and
Swallow me down ——

The flesh, your food. What's left, the soul
Yield to the red-painted maw
Of that voracious shark that glides
The deeps we crept from long ago.

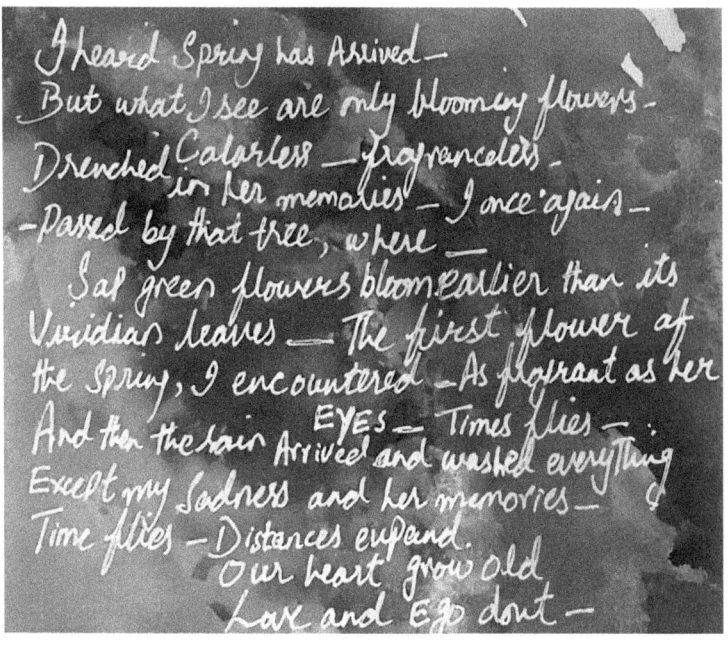

I Heard Spring Has Arrived, 2017 (Dr. Syed Tariq Shah)

*Birthday*

I worry our emotions, and that silence
That's so hard to break, conceal too well
The small, short-living essences of life
That flit away and leave us all too soon.

They hide in deep green, slumbering mountain vales
Until the seasons' wheel brings Autumn round.
We lift the latch and urge them out to dance
And fall with us like red-veined, coppered leaves.

*See*

O see, see what I have got
For you; a night, a plane
That is in turbulence
Dizzy dizzy, a star river revolving
A pound of silk curtain,
And mine, a pair of fevered eyes

## Under Seongsu Bridge

I shouldn't tell when people ask
Or blurt to every curt request.
Better throw what's me away.

Now someone's inching close to me
And I'm not close to my doves' cot.
Too far by far to hear them coo.

My heart filled up with sorrow, but
Spring water sloughed my skin, and I
Became a stone that can't be rocked.

Dove, which rock for perch and trough?
I've waited long for time that's ours
An instant that outlasts the world.

Stone-still under Seongsu bridge, its
Verdant green and iron spans.
Will even one love find me there?

*Like a Certain Night*

On a certain night in moonlight glow, you
Stepped out barefoot on the twilit path.
Your florist passed a cigarette; you lit
And kissed out smoke rings pale as nebulae.

As clouds traverse galactic spiral arms
They drifted out of your sight and from mine
While your gaze fastened upon me, and I
Wished on that orange star named for Arcturus.

My night-wide eyes looked long, long, long.
Our sadness, curled like Disque Bleu smoke around
The branches of our withered maple tree
Will never fade while you still hold it tight.

*North Bank*

Let me settle, lie at length upon
The north bank that your river-tears have made.
Sweet-bread memory, let it flow and ripple
Quiet as the murmurings from your sleep.

Though my eyes brim with tears estuarine
That drop like summer meteors: I'm not one
To gaze past you to see the southern bank; and
Far less pass you on the other side.

Your naiad's dream is all that I can see.
Coursing narrows, deeps' and shallows' frowns,
Early morning sunlight on green reeds,
Pale moonlight in the gloaming on the weirs.

No grief to live a life on that lone bank
Cherishing yellow roses of Japan.
For living there is living in your heart
Loved until its distant springs run dry.

| WHITE CROW |

*Just Before Many an Autumn*

Let life be soft
As lakes in violet gloamings.
Leave summer days to memory
Scorching suns forgot.
The singer's notched voice shivering flesh
Easy as a bird's wing feathering waves
Fading into time.
Let nights be long, filled with fragrances of orris and wormwood
The sonnets of a Portuguese nun
At autumn's door.
Drink wine brewed to the secret recipe for living
And tell none.
Keep all that sweet mystery
Have your heart beat red then blue
And conjure my tears for you.

*Recipe for Living*

She told me her private recipe for life —
*Whisky, watermelon syrup and Martini.*
Whisky from winter
Watermelon from summer
Martini not gin-and-vermouth
But misery and thrills.
The proportions she kept to herself.
How could I get so drunk yet swim
Wriggling, fish-gilled
Never sinking?

*How I Do Love Thee*

As salt and sugar, seersucker
Softness of infant skin and puppy fur
As firm faith that leaps from rocky bluffs.
As sunlight and sun-heat suffusing my body
Vermilion afterglow sparkling on lake-waves
Lines apparating from my writer's pen.
As a star's eye gleams slyly towards her old neighbour
Tipping her wineglass for loves long gone dark
As the light years I see piercing autumn dusks fading
As comets loop Sun swooping back to black homes.
As wild date-palms sway
Below the Moon and jewel-box stars.

Dear Gazelle, 2014 (Dr. Syed Tariq Shah)

*Spiral Galaxy*

Hid in the whirlpool, its dead centre.
Love and lusts take shape in her like globular clusters
But all for show.
Draw close, she grants you leave
Permissions, but none for her secret places.
Look in her eyes, tumbling in gravity
Unsuspecting. She weighs your conjectures.
Turning through one galactic night, you may become secret.
Her tender eyes tenderize your heart
Sooth your soul among the birthing stars.
Does anything matter more?
She is gas-glowing nebulae
Folded in dark since the cosmic germ split
And light flared. She walks on the upside-down sky
Cloud-blowing before the wind between the stars.

I spied her from my perch in this one spiral arm
For an instant, one turn of this stone round its miniature Sun.
In the clock-tick it took to decide
To love or not
The galaxy wheeled her to another woman's gaze.

*Crescent*

She now walks in bliss with me
In winter dusks
In darkening clouds
She transforms, bone-white crescent in my eye
A sampled heart
Glows in this lightless creeping wood
That bleeds blue grey.

Blue, grey.
From collisions I evaded
From strangers strange to me
And one familiar garden where
Her pain burns that much less.

No wind here.
Trees that flank the road are withered
Steel-blue perching magpies swoon
Like blue-grey hills give up their song.

So much that matters little
Has its worth because of her.

And I should fade and be no more
In mist receding
Burning as the gold sun climbs
If she would stand tall on a friend's red tiles
Still as a rock
White, sparkling bright
As if she'd fled
The ruin of the Cities of the Plain.

## *A Girl*

I saw you across the street, spilling promise
As my gaze fed on you
Ignoring the coming cold crowd, your look the match of mine.
Nearing, you divulged your truths
That cleaved tight to my way.
Now settling in bars to schooners of beer
To chase the Drunk a while
Memories lean on me, talking of you
And dreams of secret lands
In long numb winters.
Your currents run deep
I swear
if I'd closed my eyes, I'd have sought the crowd
Fled your indifference to me.
You could have drawn my dream, you claimed
Painted all my worries over
But no.

You wrecked them, sandcastles on a breezing strand
But I still clutch delusions
Dark crimson lips entwining my brain.
There's no escape
Heart inured to storms, though once my boat near drove upon the shore
I can't escape a promiser of promises all wrong
The alcohol unmoors me, but
Somewhere in the house the centre's stilled
No way to smooth the furrow in my soul
Only in the silly fumbling of first sight
Love I freely breathe.
Seeing you
Warmer here than your iced eyes
I'll know, and stay beyond the spell I thought
Learning sedentary toil
Carrying still that Chaos girl
Merry as girls go, always and ever.

*One Thousand Islands*

One thousand islands aren't worth your eyes.
They never cry
They hold night after night their sea-wind breaths
While Sun dives deep.
They clasp still trunks
Under nodding palms
Whispering, lying together in shared dreams
Not sinking as the Moon floats down.

What's the heart I have
I wonder
Drowning in your eyes.
A magic lake whose spells
Catch travellers in its winter frosts
Its thousand islands
Casting runes
On sluggish emerald swell.

Once so far and now so near
I wonder why
My heart beats slow
And no voice in the world will tell
Why crescent moons trace out your brow
Holding, folding
Not comparing
With your thousand isles.

*Sugar Woman*

My sugar woman
Sitting somewhere in a dim-lit corner
True?
Or drinking Bailey's
In a Wenzhouness bar with our old friends
Is that you?

Face flushed
I see, what work one sip of wine does do.

Your face burns cool
While outside others
Savour evening chill.
Cold, the still like calm my heart long held
I wish I held no more.
I could reach and touch.

Sweet wordless woman
Your sway sugars pills of time.


Here, there's that ceramic singer with his little boy
Hear, hear them sing.
Feeling you melt here with me
The world hurts less tonight.

*To the One There*

I eat green to live
A simple kind of living as anyone can see,
Green grass dew-glistening.
I don't eat much
But I drink deep
And love, love deep
Deeply love just one.
You could eat me, every part
As all his love-pets do for him
If love feeds you
And swells your heart with joy.

*Green Cherries*

She wants, she knows, she tasted first
And spied out colours in our parting glass.
For me, no taste.
It drained in.
I saw colours I remembered I imagined
Old-town brown, skyscraper blue.
She said the greatest beauty's light.
I imagined I recalled
A lustrous touch on my bared skin
Seen with my heart and scarcely real.
For instant past
I drank
A cherry beer
Seeing you green
Through thrice-fired glass.

*Sadness*

Sadness collects all over.
Say you are a fan of coffee – or not.
But you do drink it, you know, and coffee's good in its place.
Often no better than fine, but here and there's a café that you blunder in, sitting pickily and ordering like a lady, cups bitter enough to make the tastebuds quit.
However, wherever, whatever you catch in the moment flees the next.
No cup ever drunk twice so you may miss one, good and proper.
It dwindles away, turns and swells near, can never be held again. Sad fineness.
Happy and sad both. Add a dash of happy, sprinkle a little sad.
Fine sadness.

## *In My Timber's Heart*

In my timber's heart
There stands a guard
Where cluster unmined diamonds
Of the brightest blue.
There at nightfall gather
Lorn crowds of the Lost.
Though seldom I intrude
At every time I stay
My heart cries out.
The sapphire beams
Those diamonds flash
Flush out the tears
And not the milling strangers.
Were those white stones
In white bright day
Would they shine late
Like dawn-caught Moons?
And those lost crowds
Do they cry too
Fumble for love
The ways I do?

*Orange Guitar, Green Guitar*

Orange guitar, green guitar
My strummed heart
And rasgueado voices
Shake this tender April night
Despite which my glazed eyes see nil
Until
A woman starts to dance.
Pretty, bold, her man
Flat-footed at their wine-stained table.
Alone
Before
Barefoot.
Long, sinuous back to me, she seems
The imprint of a reveller
Made long years before
Dancing so I've drawn my final breath.
A black swan dance,
A feather floating free
Every chord struck
On my slack-tuned heart.

## *How Do I Slip to This Place?*

How do I slip to this place?
Craning to hear some last note from my heart
Craving tears with you.
But where are you, the heart that fled?

We were bound in flowering vines
Now far from sight and mind.

I hear a singer lilt an air
That life goes on
Until the day the soul calls back no more
And I call you.
At times I feel the drawing-down of life
Like wine
I feed my heart with your red jewel.

Eyes welling up
The singer in his song
Like one I loved, he came to peace.
I see him still
And those cruel dwellers in my garden's leaves and stalks
I see them too.

*Love Amazes Me*

Love amazes me.
Consciousness like bugs eats silence out of life.
She's there
She sees me here, no space to hide or flee.
Hush.
She's talking, hinting at the door
Where Agares will come.
I don't see, but
The way she talks attracts,
Her flickering mind attracts,
Dragging me to ocean deeps.
No handholds here.
I fall.

*In Her Dream*

In her dream
So much has wilted
A grey doe appears.
Stars dig deep in rich wet earth
But even so it's summer,
Cool, green, and mild.
My wild heart sees the flowing river stilled
Will whisper hemlock secrets in her ear
To join with her in sleep.

If she would hear she'd understand
Her beauty grows with years.
It rent my breast an age ago
And I believe, a fool's belief
That there's a mending to be had.
She raided memories and fears
Confessing to no stole-draped priest.
But I, an infidel, require

A true believer's shriving prayer
A curate's smile
And penitence.

If she would hear she'd understand
How I confess
Afraid, in gloom, alone in silence
Feeling enemies' eyes.
Hating hiding that I have
No answers to his questions.
Hating standing, still I stand
While rains pour down, and God walks on
The pathways through his dripping Garden
Tiring at last of what He's made
To clamber to familiar Heaven.
I to mine, to lie beside
Her slumbering body breathing sighs
Dreaming that she dreams of me.

*Sullen When a Summer*

When a summer loses sway
And rainfall on the islands dries
And breezes tug at fallen trees
And far from here a poet
In his Lisbon loft
Sighs out a last, long rhyming breath.
A new, small voice spreads out somewhere
A questing beast treads tree-barred paths
I listen, straining
Heeding still
That you drive through Vancouver nights.
I see, still clasping summer's sway
Like others passed through your short life
Before my brimming eyes.

*He Is a Boy*

He's that boy.
If I dreamed up
A Da Lat lover
He it would be.
He watched me smoke a cigarette
In Da Lat Railway Station
Down to the filter, then
He moved to snare my eye.

A pink rose in one slim hand
Matched with me like a magazine shoot.

He said, *Beautiful*.
Of course, I said
The station is a picture.
He shook his head
One turn, and told me, *You*!
I smiled and he smiled fiercely back

Charming, wolfish, innocent
Evening sun on heart-shaped face.

When the dawn flared
I saw again his amber skin
Ached to swallow the Da Lat sun
With one last kiss.

*Be a Visitor*

Be a visitor
Leave a heart here.
Listen, listen to a song
Sadder than the Fiddler's Green
And hear me tell my tale.
Peer inside
A gingerbread house, cry on its sunflower rows.
Those orange faces
Whoever touches even one
Catches every ray Sun shone
Clambering up the sky.

The June House, 2016 (Dr. Syed Tariq Shah)

*Name*

Your name was on my lips again
As I picked up a pen
Starting a letter to an old friend
Your name, gouged on my breast.
How to call you, write you
One last time
Watching through the still Spring night?
I lay me down and seal my eyes
Memories catch me
Memories bind me.
If they meant well
They'd catch the Spring,
Leave me drinking well alone
In that tavern of old stone
And leave me write your name.

*Spring Fever*

It's now and then a cold
Now and then a fever
Spring Fever that makes me
Yearn for Old Spring.
A flavour I defied
That's green
And fresh, so fresh it can't be real
Not even in green memory,
That never was my taste.
Though once upon a time I wished
It would be so someday.
That green leaf bears the name you do
Tender as my heart.
How could I truly flee?
From what I see but now and then

And then at last forever,
Spring Fever,
And break free
Seeing you here.
When people say it's just
Routine phenology,
I let it go
And follow on.

*You May Just Need a Few Dollars*

Just a few dollars feed my mouth
But not my ravenous gold-digger heart.
Water
Words
Orange sun glow, and rainfall
A tender kiss to wake
And walk with her above the noon.
A warm embrace for every time
We're out and back
Drink, sweet talk beside the hearth.
Reading her true
And never false
And now and then a letter.
Look deep.
Hold her as we beat out time
To mark the passing seasons.
Smile and cry with her
And conjure her a sapphire dream

Dance her to a mermaid's song
Waltz her into pale moonlight
And when you tire
Close her eyes
And wake her
When she sleeps too deep.

*Sway*

That clumsy drinker
That just drank your eyes straight down
Seems she found the Fount of Youth
Dancing man-free in the soundless crowd.
Drop the once-bit waxberry
Back to the china plate.
Leave the table, dance with her
One step closer in.
Arms tight round her waist
Sway the world with her lithe form.
Don't look down in those black eyes.
Just feel rhythm, fumbling heart
And draw her green night heat
Deep inside you.

## *She Likes This Place*

She likes this place
Would like to stay.
So much alike with my strong heart
In look and feel, I wonder if
She really knows it all.
But I may stay, learn how to speak
To speak with only her.
Write her poems, steal her dates
From high-piled, red-striped market stalls
And buy her sugared ice.
Watch her blow
Blue Lucky smoke
Do what I know
I'll love to do
Again, again, again.

*Something in*

Something in my heart, I flow it out in tears
Something in my eye, I seal it in a vein.
Some things I keep
For you, just you.
My love, say something
Or say nothing
Or leave me for a while
To talk with someone else before
I come straight back to you.
Let me slip quiet through a secret garden's wall
Bring you a love-token.
And
Tell you in the flower-shop,
Breathing with closed eyes
Of fragrance that blows
And mantles cunning faces.
And
An orange flower that I buy
For you for in its slim vase.
Keep it long, my love
The art of my something.

*Su*

Under an open sky of sailboat clouds
Disdaining all the traumas of the world,
It's floating islands that you see; for me
Twin russet moons that light your abyss eyes.

Open wide your book, and read it while
Rough snowfall layers the windows and the sills.
Grateful for red fire that routs the cold,
Settled as a dog-fox in its den.

More than every orange the world's repealed; the
Kindliness and bluntness I evince.
Doubt that summers never glow like these
Under their blue-domed, oceanic skies?

| MESCALERO |

*Ice Fall*

Clouds' waters fall
On frozen ground and white tree-tops of nearby silent groves.
Bold red squirrels
Watch us come close.
Cold breezes shiver walking souls
Kiss strangers in my breath, swirl back to me.
In my thought-world I heard
Clouds' waters drip slow from tiled roofs,
Saw you over a rain-washed cornfield.
Waters gutter on the biased edge of where I stop
Uncaught, soon to swell as ice
And freeze the past
Until it gels and cracks. Your ice-blue eyes
Feast on my fiery heart and tumble into shards.

*Prepare*

He says *Prepare some-thing*.
So, I prepare, gently as
A plucking on a nylon string
And everything thereon sounds its natural note.
Everything kissed, as how all things begin
I listen hard. What to prepare,
For him, for whom?
For rainy night
For gale-swept afternoon
I make a plan for every one.

That love will set foot on my shore
To drink dark coffee here tonight
But he won't fool the wiser me.

Fools and strangers say, *prepare*
I've nurtured, loved since I was young.
Others drinking wine I drink
Don't lose their wits and see more clear
That all I like
Is cast away.

I've waited long
Since we were parted
Late flowers bloomed in August there
And bloom here too.
Today I watched the May breeze shake them
Knew my heart remembers well
So, I'll get ready for his leaving
Or quit first, before he turns.

Memories whisper, soon the dark.
As one last night is best
Supplanting the most beautiful
I dearly wished so, turning eyes from fullness
Trading warmth for solitary cold.

Brew dark coffee for your old love
Ripe to hear the same sad tales
And bury them
With fresh-cut grass and lead-grey tears.

Prepare for winter threatening
In darkening skies beyond the shore.
Conjure up eye-shaking will
Resist the black cat's yellow glare.
Prepare to see a rainbow tree
Above the Capricorn
Board a rattling boxcar train
With locomotive breath.
Prepare to feel mosquitoes' ire
Burn for your next lover who
Will crack your heart anew.
The most venial sin.

Prepare to live in someone's dream
Of pain
And heavy loads
Unbearable lightness
And bright souls fallen to this dusty Earth.

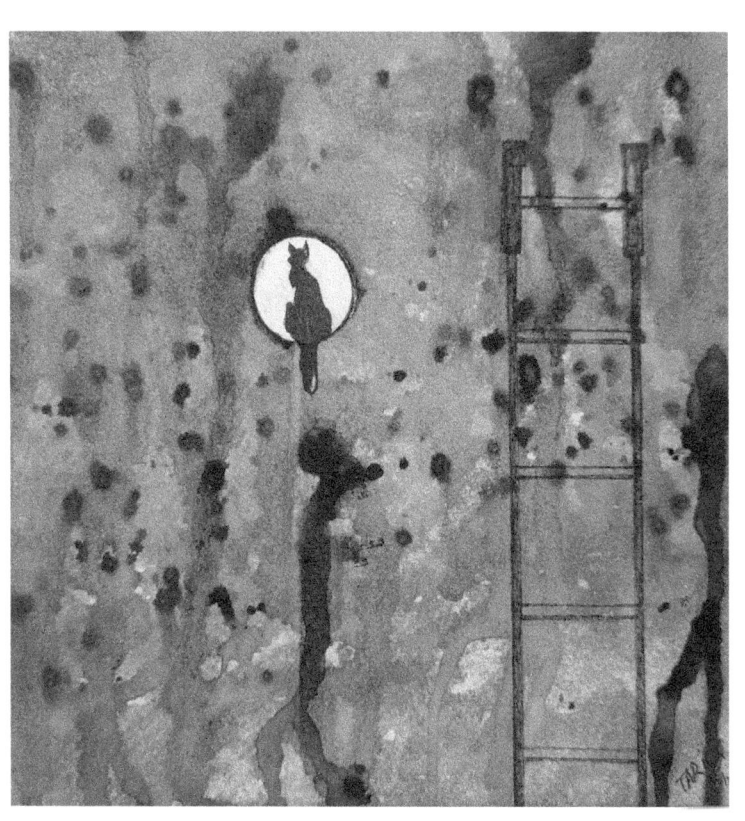

Tanzanian Coffee Aroma, 2015 (Dr. Syed Tariq Shah)

*Banana Trees*

Kids, those banana trees in silence
Those windows wiped to blue
Those doors of two kinds
Wide and shut.
They leave them as they are
Ignore them.
They see the sky's stars flicker out
Biting their lips
Creasing my heart.

*On the Mountain Road to the Village*

Seeing an insect crawling on the road
I stepped wide – no wish to hurt.
Seen closer, it's no hexapod.
A withered, splintered leaf.
A joke played on my too-soft heart.
If a man saw me so low
Would he step wide, not wish to hurt?
Maybe, for kind heart or good eyes.
Alas, those dreams in silent hiding.
What if they were stepped upon
Withered things with severed strings?
Shall I bury my heart here
When night draws down
Desolate, walking no further
Up the mountain road.

## *How Are You This Night?*

Beloved, how
Are you this night?
How are you when dusk rain falls
And slows, and stops?
I'm turning colour, white and blue
As someone flies insane.
The outline of the night gets blurred
I can't hold on
Nor hum a song
Nor see your eyes
Nor hear your heart.
Can you still stop?

Botanist
I listened to you.
Yet I can't tell
Three plants apart
Every one green as the rest.

How to dress myself as one
Flitter and shiver in brisk winds
How to die and smile?
I haven't found the way.


Doctor
I swallowed down your dry word pills
Wishing to be gulped myself like
Lady Nimue.
Calm was so much water and
I never thought to think how much
My calm love loved for me.
Dreading now my heart will flag
Owing you a better tale
Needing more wounds
Than healing hands.

*So Far, So Far*

So far, so far
Colours of memories
Cobalt through viridian.
Blazes that I battled from winter through to summer night
Still visible and visible
Like dead moons' lights
Shining out on tideless seas
And your skin
In a long, dishonestly endless dream
Wherein I'll die.
Before I take that long last step
My heart would visit yours
Just one more time.

## When It Is a Lonely Night

When it is a lonely night
Wills are uncontrolled.
Colours slip their leads, glow free
With vegetable consciousness.
Sole as a star in crystal black
Goes your random heart.

I suppose night's fallen now
Hills and trees are liquefied
Slow in their charcoal flows.
I see a man who swallows milk
Before his curtseying little girl
In my long, lonely nights.

Cherish solitude and see, I pray
How I'm still fey
And urge my beaten heart to love,
To seek wills that defy control.
Cinnabar and chlorophyll
And warmth from dimming stars.
I ache to hug the breath from you.
Will it comfort you, or me?

*A Remorse*

Beloved, has your blood
Stopped running in your veins?
Your mind puréed?
I see remorse rise in your eyes
Tears welling that both I and you
Held fast for half a summer
until now and here in that deep night
Where all things lustre clear.
But could you mourn
Just one short night
Longer, if you please?
Singing this wordless song with me
Drain the cold glass and dance with me
Fall into the deepening sea
With me clutched tight to you.
Mind that I love
I've seen you through, seen myself too
I beg you, never calculate

It's hard to leave that matchless woman
Harder still to stay, and still
Hardest of all in liminal cleft.
Mind that I love
How I regret, how I relieve
The pain of our entwining that
No heart could bear alone.
Look away
From ink stained in my neck and breast
From bowl point nib that slit my heart.
Crimson ink and youth and vigour.
Red colour of my long remorse
Made bright for you
The tint of oceans
Where sharks slide.

*1984*

1984, I miss you.
Thought I could, in memory
In histories whose various worlds
Flared coal-fire orange and powder blue
Revolving and revolving when
Life lit your eyes with gaseous flame
And you were fallen Babylon.
One cup of sweet brass wine to drink
An emerald for talisman
One mystery,
Two.
My heart still hunting.

## I Want to Cry Here Every Morning

I want to cry here every morning
For a hundred lengthening years
Till amber eyes see oceans' floors.
One hundred years of certitude
Spring tides of misery endured
While your salt kisses buoy me up.
No fear
That morning wind will chill
For you beside me fires my blood
Healer.
My healer, my mender
Bleed me, cry me whole.

## *1982*

Standing on green cotton rocks
I watched clouds climb the muslin sky
Shelter for me.
Like a tear of molten gold
That smiling man plucked out my heart
Of course, I stayed.
Drinking wine and waiting for
The cumulus to summit
And the sun to light the scarp
His face and mine.
I'd no choice but to stay.
1982
That green cotton boy
Departed Pamukkale
And traced my breadcrumb trail.
1982
I shed a salt marsh of hot tears
Wept Izmir's Sea,

Sad as they come.
I waded in, no other course
No other but to cry and dance
With him
And leave and lose.
If I could live this short life twice
I'd live it longer next time round.
I never clasped a brighter jewel.

## As a Losing Touch

As he said
It gets in blood
And as he said
There's no escape.

As he said
My place, a mess
All mine.
I got drunk from its sweet name
Melted it in caramel.

Honey mine
My caramel town
I'm in your heart
Gone with the dawn
To meet that light-foot man who looped
A flower garland round my neck,
And drink and join the throng.

Closing my eyes
Eying my close
I try to see you as you were.

If I was sweet as sherbet ice
Dessert from hot, desert sand
Would you bite me
A losing touch
And kiss the nectar from my hand?

*The Poem a City Wrote to Me*


Sigh deep.
This is me
I'm going through good people fast.
I'm losing you
But glad to know, and happy that
I'll never not have been with you.
You're the one that will be missed
The one who's like my second city
Always close to me and mine
I see you summing up my kind
Sentimental, giving, kind.

Loving and beloved so much
Making life with every breath.

Benimle Kal, we sing for you
Salt on your dish, rose petals on
The varnish of the boards you tread.
Passion scattered, dandelion seed

Fragrance for a year and day.
You'll soon depart
Beloved.
You know my life went often wrong
But one pure song I'll sing tonight.

I am what I am
Loving much
First and last one of my own
Living life in every breath.
Half my heart in Istanbul
I'll never take it home.
From far away you're just as real
My life, my people, Istanbul
Beautiful as minarets
Ugly without you, time to time
Believe me that I'll always sing
Out from here
To you.

*Beautiful, My Beautiful Woman*

Tonight, recall
Just this one word
Forget it all and drink pale wine
Thinking of just you.

Beautiful, my
Beautiful woman
You dropped me here, left me for dead.
But even so
Your unreal after-image glow
Bears me up in life, and eases
My heart through long days and nights.
I don't blame,
I don't blame you
And in the hubbub of the night, like now
Singing in Dorian mode a tune of days
Yours and mine both
That die away.

What fate, that we collided in our salad days
Now leaching out our youth apart.
My beautiful woman
The sum of all the world's bright life
No match for how you look.
Singing from my fever dreams
An anthem of our time
I pray my days are notched to yours
Till I lay down beneath green grass
And cemetery birds' laments.
Mourn with me our sundered tale
And think on us a while.

## Well, Hello There

Well, hello there.
How have you been?
I want to talk before
This massacre begins.
Before my heart greets falling night and earth
I want to hear a long-lost song,
Sharing a cigarette with you.
Refuse me not, my lovely friend
Sincerely, come.
In bacchanal we'll dance till we
Forget our names and where we live.
See no evil, hear none, do none.
My beautiful friend
See my eyes see you and bleed
Profusely, profusely.

*Elegy*

Sing an elegy for me, lover
Stroke dry blades of grass from my bleached hair.
Pluck stars from curtained night and press them to my breast
Draw the twilight shades for me
Let my body sleep.

Cry just once for me, for
Births and deaths of seasons
Plaintive and short
Spring.
Everything I once clasped tight
She left me to Fall.

Lover, never think to blame
The spring that flits away
The green that no more lights my eyes.
I still love her

As I love you.
Love
When life's illusions turn to true
And life's long river runs into
Andromeda, that galaxy
Hiding in another's stars
Then you can forget me.

*It Was Fascination*

It was fascination, and scorching sun
Leaf-green worlds
Unsheltered sky.
It was tears stumbling down, evaporating soon
Coiled mountain roads
I chose to whirl along
Back and forth, again, and then
And close again
To choosing Death.
Resistance,
That I never knew.

*It Was Fascination 2*

It was fascination
Now it's solitude.
That kinked spring my fingers brush
Moist eyes my own eyes see
Not bearing one more breath or word,

Hardly then my heart resists
Attachment of long, fervid years
To you, to you my dear.

Thirsty to drink
Walking to slake, a country mile
On that wild towpath
Often looking back.
That's the cream of life
From castle through enchanted forest
Through the dusk to mother night.

Dear one
It's been long
And still, it's fascination.
My fingers dab wet eyes of Spring
As flowers and sadness grow.

## With a Soul I Got Drunk

With a soul I burned, scorched in sunrays
Hurt and sorrowed, wept where I could lean.
Cry, cry, cry.
A tearful baby in my arms
I cried along.
Rock, rocking, beads on brows
A rattling memory projector hissed and smoked.
I drew her heart to beating on mine
With soul, with a soul
As the world folded up.
There, the place I named for Rolan
There, a face that dims and glows
There, I weigh my hues in scales
Yearning for
Red dressing more than lilac wine
Seeking truth, now I go blind
This soul and I
Become so sober, cruelly sober
Till we breathe no more.

Old Neighbor, 2016 (Dr. Syed Tariq Shah)

## *Cilia*

Oh, be gentle
Elegant
Be a zesty playboy.
Be a thief
Be rude as a plumber, or
Talk like my grandma
With her trumpet in her ear.
Oh, be busy as a shoemaker
With no time for gossip
Strong as a dark-skinned
Haddock-reeking fisherman.
Be a two-handed drinker
Smoking like a campfire,
A painter mixing
Madders and umbers – never blue.
A botanist, no chemist though

Kind lover, or
Humanitarian.
Be floating when
Shy clouds drift shyly near
Touching her eyebrows
Attending her caring heart.

*Mescaline*

Mescaline.
Like you disappeared from brilliant sunset flares
Dreams drowning down on ocean floors.
Greek chorus singing that
All dreams at long last once come true
Dragged me to the swell that swallowed me whole.
No breath, heart airless
Your eyes blind, ears deaf to hear
Goddamn, ah, God-damned.
My one wish
For one sleek fish
To make me food, all but these calyx ears
Souvenirs for you.
My body blazes
In old, gold, westering sun
Over the jelly-cold water.
Remembering I called you Lin
The others Mescaline
Slips me over the foam.

*Obsession*

Eat, Eat
But men's mind and soul
Eat, Eat
But women's body, mind and soul
But one form of pertinacious bigotry
The most seductive silence lies -
In the darkness
In the heart of the forest
While walking and crossing -
Patches of ample berries
I see, my hunger, my thirst
And there's this war,
I get to fight

*Evening*

Evening, you hold our Moon with tenderest care
Whether she's full, or half, or shadowed horn.
You let the world be palely lit by her
In colours that I jealously call mine.

But have you never tired, forgot a name, while
Ever green, you breathe the dusk to dark?
Old wine, new bottle, every close of day
You bid Her drink: new glass, new house, new love.

All my heart's an open book for you.
My thoughts, less so; how could you know that when
Our drowning sins have dyed the oceans red
For Her alone I'll offer up my prayers.

*Marguerite*

A scent of female, and a taste
For which one sweet night won't suffice.
Not even if the Moon was slowed
And dawn prolonged ten score of days.

The sugarsack's lips open wide.
The leaves of Ceropegia wood
Outside the window undulate
And whisper, ardent strings of hearts.

Now drink cold, bitter coffee, dried
In Tanzania's *kusi* winds.
Caress her beating lion's heart
And bare white teeth to bite and feed.

Coffee Cup, 2018 (Dr. Syed Tariq Shah)

*Autumn Equinox*

As autumn rain falls, so do leaves; and so
Do sounds fade into silence in my heart.
Soft landings there are none, and yet the Sun
Shines after rain and no leaf falls too far.

Patient, calm, I wait upon those amber
Wings that flit and linger, that once broke
My dream; they disappeared, appeared again
Coming and going like frivolous Queens of Hearts.

My only wish, that plane tree leaves should catch
Her steps to slow the withering of my heart.
I learned to speak for her, Shanghainese
Nine words I'd later say like dropping coins.

*Where Butterflies Go*

In winter, butterflies go where?
In my orange journal's pages slumber.
When they wake, go where to dance?
Upon my skin, in small gavottes.

www.ingramcontent.com/pod-product-compliance
Lightning Source LLC
Chambersburg PA
CBHW050246010526
44107CB00003B/211